MW01233952

AWARD WINNING BBQ RECIPES

EVERYTHING YOU EVER WANTED TO KNOW ABOUT BARBECUE

MARK GREGER

Disclaimer

This publication is designed to provide competent and reliable information regarding the subject matter covered. However, it is sold with the understanding that the author
is not engaged in rendering professional or nutritional advice. Laws and practices often vary from state and country to country and if medical or other expert assistance is required, the services of a professional should be sought. The author specifically disclaims any liability that is
incurred from use or application of the content of this book.

TABLE OF CONTENTS

INTRODUCTION

This collection of grilling recipes is sure to spark your imagination.

We've grown a lot more sophisticated with our grilling and moved beyond burgers and hot dogs.

This cookbook including Delicious barbecue recipes built around bringing out the flavor of the meat with detailed instructions and easy-to-follow steps

Let's not forget the memorable side dishes to complete your barbecue feast

These recipes are created so everyone can enjoy the flavor and ease of grilling without a lot of fuss or mess. Now, even the cook can take it easy and enjoy an afternoon or evening relaxing and being part of the fun. So, sit back, browse the recipes and start planning what to cook next.

It only takes about 10–20 minutes to heat and get the grill ready for cooking.

Whether you cook with a simple charcoal grill on your apartment balcony or have the luxury of a complete outdoor patio kitchen.

How to check the grill temperature?

For the smaller items like kebabs, burgers, hot dogs and skewers you can grill at high heat

If you can hold your hands just above the grill for 5 sec then it is low heat. And if you can hold it only for a sec then it is high heat.

This holds for both gas and charcoal grill.

But in this case you will have to constantly watch the food and turn it so that it does not burn.

For grilling the larger items and the bone-in pieces, you need to control the heat.

So you must go for medium heat.

Tips: Always keep the grates of the grill clean, Oil the food properly. Do not use spray water bottles to control flare ups, instead, move the foods to some other part of the grill when a flare up occurs.

Cooking got simpler and more comfortable, which gave even newbies a chance to grill, bake, and roast.

HERBED APPLE FLAVOR GRILLED CHICKEN

Serves 8

Ingredients

- 1 cup apple jelly
- 2 tablespoons thinly sliced thyme
- 1 tablespoon thinly sliced basil
- 4 tablespoons low-sodium soy sauce
- 2 tablespoons grated ginger
- ½ teaspoon fresh ground black pepper

Instructions

1. Put the apple jelly, thyme, basil, soy sauce, ginger and pepper in a saucepan and beat them together.
2. Heat the saucepan at medium-high heat on your grill.
3. Take to a boil.
4. Cook at the same heat for 3 minutes.
5. Stir constantly.
6. Now, remove the saucepan from the grill and keep the glaze aside to cool a little.
7. Place the chicken pieces on the grill at medium-high heat.
8. When about 3 minutes of grilling the chicken is left, brush the glaze on the pieces.
9. Grill for 3 minutes.
10. Transfer the pieces to a plate and brush them again with the glaze.
11. Cover the plate loosely with foil.
12. Serve after 5 minutes.

SWEET ORANGE GRILLED CHICKEN

Serves 8

Ingredients

- 2 tablespoons canola oil
- ½ cup pure maple syrup Zest of 2 oranges, grated
- 2 quarts orange juice
- 4 tablespoons thinly sliced thyme
- 2 tablespoons low-sodium soy sauce
- 2 teaspoons coarsely ground black pepper
- 2 thinly sliced red onions Chopped cabbage, for garnish

Instructions

1. In a saucepan, cook the canola oil at high heat.
2. Put in the thinly sliced onions and cook for 4 minutes.
3. Now, add the thyme, orange zest and juice.
4. Take to a boil. Boil for about 30 minutes until the mixture becomes thicker.
5. Stir occasionally.
6. Transfer the mixture to a bowl and mix the maple syrup, soy sauce and pepper in it.
7. Beat the mixture and then keep it aside to bring to room temperature.
8. Meanwhile, grill the chicken pieces on the grates at medium-high heat.
9. When about 2 minutes of grilling is left, brush the glaze on the pieces.
10. Grill for 3 minutes.
11. Transfer the pieces to a plate and brush them again with the glaze.
12. Cover the plate loosely with foil. Wait for 5 minutes.
13. Garnish with cabbage and serve.

HERBED LEMON FLAVOR BONELESS CHICKEN

Serves 8

Ingredients
- ½ cup olive oil 6 garlic cloves, grated
- 4 tablespoons fresh thyme, chopped Zest of 2 lemons, grated
- Juice of 2 lemons
- A pinch of salt 2 teaspoon coarsely ground black pepper
- 4 pounds boneless chicken pieces Lemons, for garnish

Instructions
1. Put olive oil, garlic, thyme, lemon zest and juice in a bowl and mix.
2. Soak the chicken pieces in the marinade and cover the bowl.
3. Put the bowl in the refrigerator for about 3 hours to marinate.
4. Take the bowl out from the refrigerator and sprinkle with salt and black pepper evenly throughout the chicken pieces.
5. Grill the marinated chicken at medium-high heat until it becomes brown.
6. Garnish with lemons cut in half and serve.

VINEGAR-ROSEMARY CHICKEN BARBECUE

Serves 8

Ingredients

- 8 tablespoons olive oil
- 4 onions, chopped 2 garlic cloves, grated Zest of 2 oranges, grated
- 4 cups orange juice
- 6 tablespoons sherry vinegar
- 2 cups low-sodium chicken broth
- 4 rosemary sprigs, finely sliced
- 6 tablespoons honey
- Kosher salt and freshly ground black pepper 4 pounds chicken pieces Rosemary sprigs for garnish

Instructions

Put 4 tablespoons oil in a saucepan and cook it over high heat. Put the onions and garlic in the saucepan and cook for 3 minutes. Put the orange zest, juice and sherry vinegar into the saucepan and take to a boil. Mix thoroughly. Cook at high heat until it reduces to half the volume, for another 7-8 minutes. Stir occasionally. Mix the broth and rosemary into the mixture and simmer until it gets thick (10-12 minutes). Transfer the sauce to a bowl and combine it with honey, salt and pepper. Leave aside to cool a little. Meanwhile, place the chicken pieces (brushed with remaining oil, salt and pepper) skin side down on the grates at medium heat. Cook for 4-5 minutes. Turn the pieces over and close the lid of the grill. Cook the chicken until it is golden brown. Transfer the pieces to a plate and lightly brush the sauce on the pieces. Cover the plate loosely with foil. Wait for 5 minutes. Sprinkle the rosemary sprigs on top and serve with the sauce.

BARBECUE CHICKEN MARINATED WITH BEER

Serves 8

Ingredients
- 2 bottles extra stout beer
- ½ cup extra-virgin olive oil
- 2 tablespoon grated lemon zest
- 6 tablespoons fresh lemon juice
- 2 tablespoon finely sliced thyme
- 4 teaspoons Dijon mustard
- 8 garlic cloves, grated
- 2 teaspoons kosher salt
- 2 teaspoons coarsely ground black pepper
- 2 whole chickens, cut up

Instructions
1. Put the beer, oil, lemon zest, juice, thyme, mustard, garlic, kosher salt and black pepper in a bowl and beat the mixture.
2. Soak the chicken pieces into the marinade by thoroughly mixing in the bowl.
3. You can also use a sealed plastic bag for mixing.
4. Place the bowl in the refrigerator for at least 4 hours to marinate.
5. Now, take out the chicken pieces from the bowl and grill them on the grates at medium heat.
6. Save the left-over marinade in a cup.
7. Boil this marinade in a saucepan for 2 minutes, stirring constantly.
8. Then, keep the saucepan aside and let it cool a little.
9. Grill the chicken for about 40 minutes until the juices run clear when cut with tip of a knife. (When about 15 minutes of grilling is left, brush the marinade on the pieces. Do this once per side)
10. Transfer the pieces to a plate.
11. Serve warm.

EGG MARINADE BARBECUE CHICKEN

Serves 8

Ingredients
- 4 chickens, cut up
- 4 tablespoons of lemon juice
- 2 cups vegetable oil
- 2 eggs
- 4 tablespoons kosher salt
- 2 tablespoons garlic salt
- 4 teaspoons poultry seasoning
- 2 teaspoon fresh ground black pepper
- 4 green onions, sliced

Instructions
1. Put vegetable oil, lemon juice and eggs in a bowl and beat thoroughly.
2. Mix kosher salt, garlic salt, black pepper and seasoning and stir the mixture.
3. Soak the chicken pieces into the mixture.
4. Cover the bowl and put it in the refrigerator for at least 2 hours to marinate.
5. Take the bowl out from the refrigerator and grill the chicken pieces on the grates at medium-high heat.
6. Grill each side for about 20 minutes. (Breast and thigh pieces take longer to grill than other pieces)
7. Grill the chicken until the juices run clear when cut with tip of a knife.
8. Transfer the pieces to a plate.
9. Garnish with green onions and serve.

PARSLEY WHITE GRILLED CHICKEN

Serves 8

Ingredients

- 2 cup red wine vinegar
- 1 cup distilled white vinegar
- 2 cup pineapple juice
- 2 cup sugar
- 2 jalapeño chile, coarsely sliced
- 2 ginger pieces, grated
- 1 large red bell pepper, thinly diced
- 1 large yellow bell pepper, thinly diced
- 6 tablespoons parsley leaves, thinly sliced
- Kosher salt to taste
- 4 pounds chicken pieces

Instructions

1. Put the vinegars, pineapple juice, sugar, jalapeño, parsley and ginger in a saucepan and mix them together.
2. Cook it at medium heat and boil for about 15 minutes until the amount is reduced to half. Stir occasionally.
3. Transfer the sauces into a bowl and mix it with the peppers and salt.
4. Grill the chicken pieces on the grates of the grill at medium-high heat.
5. Grill every side until the juices run clear when cut with tip of a knife.
6. Transfer the pieces to a plate and brush them with the sauce immediately.
7. Cover the plate loosely with foil. Wait for 5 minutes.
8. Garnish with remaining parsley and serve.

SALTED CHICKEN BARBECUE WITH ASPARAGUS

Serves 8

Ingredients
- 4 pound chicken pieces, skin-on
- 8 tablespoons olive oil
- 2 bunch asparagus, ends trimmed
- Kosher salt to taste
- White pepper to taste

Instructions
1. Pre-heat your grill to a medium heat.
2. Brush the chicken pieces with olive oil (4 tablespoons).
3. Then, drizzle the salt and pepper on the chicken generously.
4. Place the pieces on the grates of the grill at medium heat and grill them until the juices run clear when cut with tip of a knife. (Keep turning the sides after every 8 minutes)
5. Transfer the chicken to a plate.
6. Cover the chicken plate loosely with foil. Wait for 5 minutes.
7. Meanwhile, mix the asparagus, pinch of salt, pepper and 4 tablespoons of olive oil in a bowl.
8. Grill the asparagus over medium heat on a grill pan until tender.
9. Take the pan off the grill.
10. Garnish the chicken with grilled asparagus and serve.

INDIAN BARBECUE CHICKEN

Serves 8

Ingredients
- 6 tablespoons vegetable oil
- 2 onions, finely diced
- 6 garlic cloves, finely grated
- 6 tablespoons ginger, finely grated
- 2 cup tomato ketchup
- 2/3 cup distilled white vinegar
- 2/3 cup tamarind paste (available online)
- 2/3 cup un-sulphured molasses
- 2 pinch sugar
- 6 tablespoons whole-grain mustard
- 1/2 teaspoon cayenne pepper
- 2 teaspoon salt
- 2 teaspoon freshly ground pepper
- 4 pounds boneless chicken pieces
- Green onions, cut in half

Instructions
1. Cook 6 tablespoons of oil in a saucepan over medium heat.
2. Add the onions to the pan and cook for 4 minutes until onion looks translucent.
3. Then, add the garlic, ginger, ketchup, vinegar, tamarind, molasses, sugar, mustard and cayenne pepper in the mixture and simmer at low heat for 6 minutes. Stir occasionally.
4. Then, take the pan off the heat and season the sauce with salt and black pepper.
5. Pre-heat the grill to medium-high heat.
6. Brush the chicken pieces with oil and season with salt before grilling.
7. Grill the pieces on the grates at medium-high heat until almost cooked.
8. Keep turning sides.
9. Now, reduce the heat to low and brush the pieces with sauce.
10. Grill for about 4 minutes and keep turning sides.
11. Transfer the pieces to a plate and lightly brush the sauce on the pieces.
12. Cover the plate loosely with foil.
13. Wait for 5 minutes. Garnish with green onions and serve.

SALTED CHICKEN THIGHS WITH CABBAGE AND TOMATOES

Serves 8

Ingredients

- 16 medium bone-in, skin-on chicken thighs (6 ounces each)
- 6 tablespoons olive oil
- Kosher salt to taste
- Freshly cracked black pepper
- 2 head white cabbages for garnish
- 6 tomatoes, chopped for garnish

Instructions

1. Pre-heat your grill to a medium heat.
2. Brush the chicken thighs with olive oil.
3. Then, drizzle the salt and black pepper on the chicken generously.
4. Place the pieces on the grates of the grill at medium heat and grill them until the juices run clear when cut with tip of a knife. (Keep turning the sides after every 8-9 minutes)
5. Transfer the grilled chicken to a plate.
6. Cover the chicken plate loosely with foil.
7. Wait for 5 minutes.
8. Serve chicken garnished with shredded cabbage and chopped tomato.

MUSTARD-OREGANO FLAVOR BARBECUE CHICKEN

Serves 8

Ingredients

- 1/2 cup coarse-ground mustard
- 2/3 cup extra-virgin olive oil
- 1/2 cup balsamic vinegar
- 6 tablespoons roughly chopped fresh oregano
- 4 teaspoons freshly cracked black pepper
- 16 medium bone-in, skin-on chicken thighs (6 ounces each)
- 6 tablespoons olive oil
- Kosher salt to taste
- Freshly cracked black pepper

Instructions

1. Put the mustard, 2/3 cup olive oil, vinegar, oregano, black pepper and salt in a large bowl and beat them together.
2. Pre-heat your grill to a medium heat.
3. Brush the chicken thighs with olive oil.
4. Then, drizzle the salt and black pepper on the chicken generously.
5. Place the pieces on the grates of the grill at medium heat and grill them until the juices run clear when cut with tip of a knife. (Keep turning the sides after every 8-9 minutes)
6. Transfer the grilled chicken to the large bowl (step 1).
7. Mix the sauce with the grilled chicken until the pieces are well covered with the sauce and serve.

HERBED GARLIC CHICKEN GRILLED

Serves 8

Ingredients
- 2/3 cup extra-virgin olive oil
- 2 tablespoons garlic, finely chopped
- ½ cup thyme, finely chopped
- 16 shots of Tabasco Juice of 2 lemons
- 6 pounds chicken pieces, cut up
- 3 tablespoons olive oil for brushing chicken
- Kosher salt to taste
- Freshly cracked black pepper to taste

Instructions
1. Pre-heat your grill to a medium heat.
2. Brush the olive oil on the chicken pieces.
3. Then, drizzle the salt and black pepper on the chicken wings generously.
4. Place the pieces on the grates of the grill at medium heat and grill them until the juices run clear when cut with tip of a knife. (Keep turning the sides after every 8-9 minutes)
5. Transfer the grilled chicken to a large bowl.
6. Add 2/3 cup oil, garlic, thyme, Tabasco and lemon juice to this bowl and mix until the chicken is full covered with the ingredients added.
7. Serve hot.

PEPPERONCINI GRILLED CHICKEN

Serves 8

Ingredients

- 2/3 cup extra-virgin olive oil
- 2 tablespoons garlic, finely chopped
- 2 tablespoons pepperoncini, minced
- 2 tablespoons ground cumin
- ½ cup fresh parsley, chopped Juice of 2 lemons
- 6 pounds chicken pieces, cut up
- 3 tablespoons olive oil for brushing chicken
- Kosher salt to taste
- Freshly cracked black pepper to taste

Instructions

1. Pre-heat your grill to a medium heat.
2. Brush the olive oil on the chicken pieces.
3. Then, drizzle the salt and black pepper on the chicken pieces generously.
4. Place the pieces on the grates of the grill at medium heat and grill them until the juices run clear when cut with tip of a knife. (Keep turning the sides after every 8-9 minutes)
5. Transfer the grilled chicken to a large bowl.
6. Add 2/3 cup oil, garlic, pepperoncini, cumin, parsley, lemon juice, salt and pepper to this bowl and mix until the chicken is full covered with the ingredients added.
7. Serve hot.

GRILLED CHICKEN SKEWERS WITH FRIED CORNS

Serves 8

Ingredients
- 1 bag (16-ounce) frozen corn, defrosted
- 4 tablespoon butter
- 3 tablespoons sugar Juice of 2 lemons
- 4 pounds boneless chicken pieces, cut into
- 1-inch chunks 6 tablespoons olive oil
- Kosher salt to taste
- Freshly cracked black pepper to taste

Instructions
1. Pre-heat your grill to a medium heat.
2. Meanwhile, melt 4 tablespoons butter in a skillet over medium-high heat.
3. Add the corn to melted butter and stir for 1 minute.
4. Add the sugar and cook for 2 more minutes.
5. Add more butter if need be.
6. Cook for 5 more minutes.
7. Add salt and 1/2 teaspoon black pepper. Keep aside.
8. Add the chicken, olive oil, salt and pepper in a large bowl and mix until the chicken is full covered with these ingredients.
9. Now, thread the chicken pieces onto the skewers closely together.
10. Cook the skewers over the grill at medium heat.
11. Roll them every 3 minutes.
12. Cook until the pieces are opaque all the way through when cut with a knife.
13. Transfer the grilled chicken to a large bowl.
14. Add the fried corn to this bowl and mix them together.
15. Serve hot.

GRILLED COCA CHICKEN

Serves 8

Ingredients

- 4 pounds chicken pieces, skinless, boneless
- 1 can of coca-cola 1 medium onion, finely chopped
- 2 garlic cloves, crushed
- 2 tablespoons rapeseed oil
- 6 large spoons of tomato sauce
- 4 tablespoons soy sauce
- 3 teaspoons chilli powder
- 2 tablespoons brown sugar
- 2 tablespoons sweet paprika
- 2 tablespoons olive oil
- Pinch of salt Bread

Instructions

1. Pre-heat your grill to a medium heat.
2. Meanwhile, put oil in a large saucepan and cook over stove for 3 minutes.
3. Add the onion and cook until it becomes translucent.
4. Add the garlic and cook for 4 minutes.
5. Keep stirring constantly.
6. Now, mix the cola, tomato sauce and soy sauce into the saucepan and simmer for 5 minutes. Stir constantly. Keep aside.
7. Add the chicken, chilli powder, sugar, paprika and cumin in a large bowl and mix until the chicken is fully covered with these ingredients.
8. Now, place the chicken pieces onto the grates of the grill at medium-high heat.
9. Turn sides after every 6 minutes.
10. When almost cooked, brush them lightly with the sauce made in step 3.
11. Grill until the pieces are opaque all the way through when cut with a knife.
12. Transfer the grilled chicken to a plate and serve with the sauce.

ASIAN FLAVORED CHICKEN BARBECUE

Serves 8

Ingredients
- 2/3 cup toasted sesame oil
- ½ cup ginger, finely grated
- 6 tablespoons garlic, finely grated
- 4 tablespoons freshly cracked black pepper
- 6 tablespoons orange zest
- 6 tablespoons dried red pepper flakes, crushed
- Hoisin sauce
- 6 pounds chicken pieces, cut up
- 3 tablespoons olive oil
- Kosher salt to taste
- Freshly cracked black pepper to taste

Instructions
1. Pre-heat your grill to a medium-high heat.
2. Meanwhile, put the sesame oil, ginger, garlic, orange zest, red pepper and black pepper in a bowl and mix them thoroughly to make the glaze.
3. Brush the chicken with olive oil.
4. Then, drizzle the salt and pepper on the chicken generously.
5. Place the chicken pieces on the grill at medium-high heat.
6. Turn sides every 7 minutes.
7. While only 2 minutes of grilling is left, brush the chicken with the glaze.
8. Grill until the chicken is opaque all the way through when cut with a knife.
9. Transfer the pieces to a plate and drizzle with hoisin sauce.
10. Serve hot with hoisin sauce.

HERBED BARBECUE CHICKEN BURGERS

Serves 4 burgers

Ingredients
- 1 pound chicken breasts, boneless, skinless
- 2 tablespoon olive oil
- 1 small carrot, finely grated
- 2 green onions, finely minced
- 2 garlic cloves, finely minced
- 2 teaspoons dried parsley
- 2 teaspoons dried oregano
- 1 teaspoon salt
- 1 teaspoon black pepper
- 1 cabbage, coarsely chopped
- 2 tomatoes, coarsely chopped
- 4 Hamburger buns, cut in half

Instructions
1. Pre-heat the grill to medium heat.
2. Put chicken breasts, oil, carrots, green onions, garlic, parsley, oregano, salt and pepper in a large bowl and mix them together.
3. Place the chicken breasts on lightly oiled grates of the grill at medium heat.
4. Turn once.
5. Allow them to cook until the chicken is opaque all the way through when cut with a knife, about 15 minutes.
6. Transfer the breasts to a plate.
7. Toast the buns on the grill or in the oven.
8. Then, place each breast piece inside a hamburger bun.
9. If some pieces are small, then place 2 pieces inside a bun.
10. Stuff the burger with chopped cabbage, tomatoes and your favorite sauce and serve.

SPINACH-MAYONNAISE CHICKEN BURGERS

Serves 4 burgers

Ingredients
- 1 pound chicken breasts, boneless, skinless
- 2 tablespoons olive oil
- 2 red onions, sliced
- 1 tomato, thinly sliced
- Fresh spinach, coarsely chopped
- 2 tablespoons mayonnaise
- 1 tablespoon chilli sauce
- 4 Burger buns, cut in half

Instructions
1. Pre-heat the grill to a medium-high heat.
2. Brush the chicken breasts with olive oil and place them on the grates at medium-high heat. Turn once.
3. Cook until the chicken is opaque all the way through when cut with a knife, about 12 minutes.
4. Transfer grilled chicken to a plate.
5. Add one tablespoon olive oil and heat it on a stove for 1 minute.
6. Then, add the onions to it and cook until the onions turn translucent.
7. Toast the buns on the grill or in the oven.
8. Stuff the buns with the chicken breasts, tomato slices, cooked onions, spinach, mayonnaise and sweet chilli sauce.
9. Serve.

KALAMATA CHICKEN BARBECUE PIZZA

Serves 1 Pizza

Ingredients
- Olive oil for brushing
- 1/2 batch food-processor pizza dough
- 1/2 cup barbecue pizza sauce
- 1 cup mozzarella cheese, grated
- 1/2 cup cheddar cheese, grated
- 1 tablespoon Kalamata olives, sliced
- 1 cup shredded cooked chicken
- 1/4 small red onion, thinly sliced
- Fresh parsley leaves, coarsely sliced

Instructions
1. Preheat the grill in such a way that the centre burner is at medium-low heat and the burners at the sides ate at high heat.
2. Take a large grill pan and brush it with olive oil.
3. Roll out the pizza dough into a 12" diameter pizza dough on a floured surface and transfer it to the grill pan.
4. Spread the barbecue sauce on the dough evenly.
5. Then, drizzle the mozzarella cheese and the cheddar cheese on it evenly.
6. Now, sprinkle the shredded chicken, onions and kalamata olives as the topping.
7. Place the grill pan in the centre of the grill at medium-low heat.
8. Close the lid of the grill.
9. Grill for about 6 minutes and until all the cheese is melted and the crust becomes crisp.
10. Take the grill pan out and transfer the pizza to a cutting board.
11. Season with parsley leaves.
12. Cut into slices according to the number of people and serve with a drink.

HONEY BARBECUE CHICKEN

Serves 8

Ingredients
- Vegetable cooking spray
- Honey Barbecue Sauce
- 4 pounds chicken pieces, cut up

Instructions
1. Coat the grates with a cooking spray and then pre-heat the grill to a medium-high heat.
2. Place the chicken pieces on the grates of the grill at medium-high heat.
3. Close the lid. (Turn the pieces once after 8 minutes.)
4. Now, decrease the heat to low and grill with the lid closed until almost cooked, about 40 minutes. (Chicken breasts take longer time to grill than other pieces.)
5. When about 10 minutes of grilling the chicken is left, brush the honey barbecue sauce on the pieces.
6. Grill for 10 minutes.
7. Transfer the pieces to a plate and brush them again with the glaze.
8. Cover the plate loosely with foil.
9. Serve after 5 minutes.

HERBED CHICKEN SKEWERS WITH MUSHROOMS AND ZUCCHINI

Serves 8

Ingredients

- 4 pounds chicken breasts, skinless, boneless, cut into chunks
- 2 yellow onions, quartered & cut into large pieces
- 30 baby portobello mushrooms, stems removed
- 4 small zucchini, cut into 1-inch rounds
- Juice of 6 lemons
- 6 cloves garlic, minced
- 4 tablespoons dried dill
- 4 tablespoon dried thyme
- 2 tablespoons dried chervil
- 6 tablespoons olive oil
- Salt to taste
- Fresh ground pepper to taste

Instructions

1. Put the lemon juice, garlic, dried dill, thyme, chervil, olive oil, 1 teaspoon salt and 1 teaspoon black pepper in a large bowl and beat them together to make the marinade.
2. Add the chicken, mushrooms, yellow onions and zucchini to the bowl and mix thoroughly.
3. Now, thread the soaked chicken, mushrooms and zucchini on a wooden skewer one after the other.
4. Cover the skewers and put them in the refrigerator for at least 2 hours to marinate.
5. Pre-heat the grill to high heat.
6. Place the skewers on the grill at high heat.
7. Use tongs to turn the skewers occasionally so that the foods are cooked evenly on all sides.
8. Cook until there is no pinkness in the chicken and the juices run clear when cut with the tip of a knife, about 18-20 minutes.
9. Use tongs to transfer the skewers to a plate.
10. Serve after 5 minutes.

BLUEBERRY FLAVOR GRILLED CHICKEN

Serves 8

Ingredients
- 3 pounds chicken breasts, boneless, skinless
- 1 cup blueberries, crushed
- ½ cup ketchup
- 4 tablespoons dark brown sugar
- 4 tablespoons apple cider vinegar
- 2 tablespoon soy sauce
- 4 garlic cloves, finely minced
- 2 red onions, finely minced
- 2 tablespoons Dijon mustard
- Green onions for garnish, cut in half

Instructions
1. Put blueberries in a saucepan over low heat and stir.
2. Wait for them to pop and when they do crush them with a masher.
3. Add the ketchup, sugar, vinegar, soy sauce, garlic, onions and mustard to the saucepan and mix thoroughly at low heat.
4. Then, simmer the marinade for 25-30 minutes at low heat until it looks thicker. Stir frequently.
5. Soak the chicken pieces in the marinade.
6. Cover the bowl and put it in the refrigerator for at least 2 hours to marinate.
7. Take the bowl out from the refrigerator and grill the chicken pieces on the grates at medium-high heat.
8. Grill each side for about 20 minutes. (Breast and thigh pieces take longer to grill than other pieces)
9. Grill the chicken until the juices run clear when cut with tip of a knife.
10. Transfer the pieces to a plate.
11. Garnish with green onions and serve.

CHERRY-CHIPOTLE CHICKEN BARBECUE

Serves 8

Ingredients

- 1½ cup fresh dark sweet cherries, pitted and chopped
- ¾ cup chicken broth, reduced sodium
- 1/3 cup cherry preserves
- ½ cup ketchup
- 1 tablespoon soy sauce
- 2 tablespoons cider vinegar
- 1½ teaspoons minced canned chipotle peppers in adobo sauce
- 1½ teaspoons dried oregano
- ¼ teaspoon ground cinnamon
- ¼ teaspoon ground cloves
- Pinch of ground nutmeg
- 3 pounds chicken breasts, boneless, skinless
- Cooking spray

Instructions

1. Put the cherries, broth, preserves, ketchup, soy sauce, vinegar, chipotle peppers, oregano, cinnamon, cloves and nutmeg in a large bowl and beat them together.
2. Add the chicken pieces to the bowl and mix until they are completely soaked in the marinate.
3. Cover the bowl and put it in the refrigerator for at least 2 hours to marinate.
4. Coat the grates with a cooking spray and then pre-heat the grill to medium-high heat.
5. Place the chicken pieces on the grates of the grill at medium-high.
6. Cook until the chicken is opaque all the way through when cut with the tip of a knife. (Keep turning sides after every 7 minutes.)
7. Transfer the grilled chicken to a plate and cover with a foil.
8. Meanwhile, transfer the remaining marinade to a skillet and take to boil.
9. Then simmer it for about 15 minutes until the sauce is reduced to half and seems thicker.
10. Serve the chicken with sauce.

GRILLED SALMON

Serves 3

Ingredients
- 1 kg fresh Salmon
- 2 tbsp brown sugar
- 1 tsp dried dill
- 1 tsp pepper
- 1 tsp salt

Instructions
1. Wash and pat dry the fish carefully.
2. You must be careful with raw fish meat because it is delicate and can break.
3. Mix the salt, pepper, sugar, and dill in a bowl.
4. Rub this sugar mixture on the top side of the fish.
5. Put it in the refrigerator for one hour.
6. This will allow the fish to dry brine.
7. Preheat the grill for medium to high heat.
8. Take out the fish and let it come to room temperature.
9. Grill the fish for 4-5 mins on each side.
10. The dish can be served at room temperature or even cold.

SPICY GRILLED CHICKEN

Serves 4

Ingredients

- 1 medium-sized whole chicken with skin
- 1 tbsp thyme
- 2 tbsp cayenne pepper
- 1 tbsp garlic powder
- 2 tbsp chili powder
- 1 tbsp salt
- 2 tbsp sugar
- 1 tbsp onion powder
- 2 tbsp black pepper
- 3 tbsp olive oil

Instructions

1. Preheat the grill for medium to high heat setting.
2. In a medium-sized mixing bowl, mix the thyme, cayenne pepper, garlic powder, chili powder, salt, sugar, onion powder, and black pepper.
3. This will make the perfect rub for the chicken.
4. First, rub the whole chicken with olive oil.
5. All sides and inside the hollow cavity of chicken as well.
6. After that, apply the prepared rub on the chicken generously.
7. Rub it on the entire surface of the chicken.
8. Put the skin over the breast of the chicken and apply the rub under the skin as well.
9. Cut the chicken into 8 pieces with a butcher's knife.
10. Grill the chicken pieces for 7 minutes on each side.
11. Served the grilled chicken warm.

GRILLED CORN ON THE COB CORN

Serves 6

Ingredients

- 6 pieces ear corn with husks
- Brown sugar
- 2 tbsp Salt
- ½ tsp Garlic powder
- ½ tsp Melted butter
- ¼ cup Onion powder
- 1 tsp Sliced green onion

Instructions

1. Take a large roasting pot and fill it half with room temperature water.
2. Pull the husks of all the corn cobs and remove the silks.
3. Let the husks remain attached to the cob but just pulled back.
4. Soak the corn cobs in the water and if needed, fill the pot with more water to completely immerse the cobs into water.
5. Soak for 4 hours.
6. After that, remove the cobs from the pot, place them on paper towels, and let them dry.
7. Preheat the grill for medium to high heat setting.
8. In a mixing bowl, mix the butter, sugar, salt, onion powder, and garlic powder to make a rub for the corn on the cob.
9. With the help of a brush, apply the rub generously to the corn cobs Grill the corn cobs for 5 to 6 minutes on each side.
10. Let them rest for 10 minutes, and then serve them as a delicious side dish.

GRILLED CHICKEN WITH ASPARAGUS

Serves 3

Ingredients
For Chicken:
- 3 to 4 pieces chicken thighs
- 5 tbsp store-bought BBQ rub water as required.
- 1 tsp sugar
- 1 tsp salt
- ¼ cup apple cider vinegar

For Asparagus
- 1 bunch asparagus
- 1 tsp red pepper flakes
- ¼ cup balsamic vinegar
- 1 tsp pepper
- 1 tsp salt

Instructions
1. Prepare to brine the chicken thighs.
2. Put the chicken in a large zip lock bag, then add Vinegar, salt, and sugar.
3. Then, fill the bag with water such that the chicken pieces are completely soaked.
4. Put it in the refrigerator for 2 to 3 hours.
5. The brining process will ensure that the chicken does not dry out while grilling.
6. Similarly, prepare a marinade for the asparagus bunch as well.
7. Please put it in a large zip lock bag.
8. Add the balsamic vinegar, salt pepper, pepper flakes, and water to soak the asparagus.
9. Please leave it in the refrigerator for 3 hours.
10. Prepare a small BBQ spray bottle having one part vinegar, two parts water, and 1 tsp sugar.
11. Mix it properly.
12. This will be used to spray on the chicken while it is being grilled
13. Take the chicken out of the refrigerator after 2 hours and wash and dry the pieces.
14. Apply the BBQ rub generously on the chicken pieces.
15. Preheat the grill for medium to high heat.
16. Place the chicken on the grill.

17. Grill for at least 10 minutes on each side with flipping occasionally.
18. Spray with the BBQ spray bottle after every 2 to 3 minutes.
19. This will prevent the chicken from drying.
20. Grill for about 15 to 20 mins.
21. Take the chicken off and let it rest for 5 minutes.
22. Meanwhile, please take out the asparagus and spread it on a paper towel, and pat dry.
23. Put the asparagus on the grill.
24. Grill for 2 minutes on each side and then take off from the grill.
25. Serve the chicken with a side of asparagus.
26. This is a good pairing to serve, and the asparagus complements the grilled chicken beautifully.

GRILLED TURKEY AND TABASCO SAUCE

Serves 3 to 4

Ingredients
- 1 piece turkey breast
- 1 piece 4 tbsp store-bought BBQ rub
- 3 tbsp olive oil
- 100 g butter
- 2 tsp hot Tabasco sauce
- 1 tsp honey

Instructions
1. First, preheat the grill for medium to high heat.
2. Next, prepare the turkey meat.
3. Cover the whole meat with a layer of olive oil.
4. Rub the oil generously.
5. Then apply the BBQ rub on the whole meat piece.
6. Rub the mixture generously so that the whole turkey breast is covered with the BBQ rub.
7. In a heatproof cup, prepare the basting mixture for the turkey.
8. Add the butter, cut into small cubes to the cup.
9. Put in the honey, hot sauce, and ¼ teaspoon BBQ rub.
10. Put the turkey and basting mixture on the grill.
11. Let the turkey breast cook for 10 to 15 minutes on each side while flipping occasionally.
12. After a while, you will see that the basting mixture is steaming.
13. Pour the basting mixture about 2 tbsp on the meat and let it smoke.
14. Repeat the procedure with the basting mixture after every 2 to 3 minutes.
15. Take off the meat from the grill when it becomes tender.
16. Let the meat rest for 15 minutes, and then slice it.
17. Serve this mouth-watering and delicious meal to your friends and family.

GRILLED POTATOES BAKED

Serves 4

Ingredients
- 4 medium-sized potatoes
- ¼ cup Olive oil
- 1 tsp granular
- Salt

Instructions
1. Preheat the grill for a high heat setting.
2. Wash the potatoes and dry them on a paper towel.
3. Poke each potato with a fork 5 or six times at different places on the potato surface.
4. This will prevent the potato from exploding when it is exposed to a high temperature.
5. Brush the potatoes generously with olive oil.
6. Season the potatoes with salt.
7. Place the potatoes near the charcoal in the grill.
8. After 45 minutes, check the potatoes for doneness.
9. When the potatoes are being cooked, you can use the grill and grate to grill other things.
10. Take the potatoes out and let them rest for 10 minutes.
11. Slit the potatoes from the entrance and fill them with American-style chili if you want to serve as a main dish.
12. Another serving idea is to slit the centre and fill it with sour cream and top it with sliced green onions.
13. This makes a perfect side dish.

GRILLED BURGERS WITH FRESH VEGETABLES

Serves 6

Ingredients
- 6 pieces pre-prepared beef burger patties
- Salt
- 2 tbsp Garlic Powder
- ½ tbsp Pepper
- 1 tbsp Dehydrated onion ½ tbsp

Instructions
1. Make sure that the burger patties are at room temperature.
2. Preheat the grill at a high-temperature setting.
3. In a mixing bowl, add the salt, pepper, garlic powder, and dehydrated onion.
4. Mix these ingredients well such that a rub is formed.
5. Apply this rub on the burger patties.
6. Cover both sides of the burger patty with the rub.
7. Grill the burger patties for 8 minutes on eat side and then set them aside for assembly.
8. Next, prepare the buns by putting them on a grill.
9. Grill the buns for one minute on each side and then assemble.
10. Assemble the burgers with fresh vegetables like onion, lettuce, and tomatoes.
11. Serve warm.

GRILLED CHICKEN DRUMSTICKS

Serves 6

Ingredients
- 1 ½ kg chicken drumsticks
- ½ cup store-bought steak rub
- 1 tsp cayenne pepper
- ½ cup BBQ sauce
- 5 tbsp Tabasco sauce

Instructions
1. Wash and pat dry the drumsticks.
2. Do not remove the skins from the chicken drumsticks.
3. Rub the drumsticks with the store-bought steak rub and the cayenne pepper.
4. Keep the drumsticks in the refrigerator for 2 hours.
5. Preheat the grill for medium to high heat setting.
6. Please take out the drumsticks from the refrigerator and wait for 15 minutes before grilling them.
7. Grill the drumstick by grilling them for seven minutes on each side.
8. Take the drumsticks off the grill and onto a plate.
9. Let the drumsticks rest for 3 to 4 minutes.
10. Meanwhile, mix the BBQ sauce and tabasco sauce in a bowl.
11. Dip all the drumsticks in the sauce one by one and arrange them on a platter.
12. Serve these delicious drumsticks to your friends and family.

GRILLED MAC WITH CREAM CHEESE

Serves 4

Ingredients
- ½ kg Elbow Macaroni
- 3 cups milk
- ¼ cup flour
- 500 g grated cheese
- 250 g Cream cheese
- ¼ cup butter
- Salt to taste
- Pepper to taste

Instructions
1. First, boil 12 cups of water in a medium cooking pot.
2. When the water comes to a boil, add the elbow macaroni, and let it boil for 8 to 10 minutes.
3. When the macaroni is boiled, remove all the water, and put the macaroni aside.
4. Next, you will prepare the cheese sauce.
5. In a medium-sized pan, put in the butter in melt it over the flame.
6. After the butter is melted, add the flour, and mix it.
7. Cook for about two minutes till the flour starts to brown.
8. Next, add the milk and cook for five minutes with constant stirring or whisking to not form lumps.
9. Let the milk thicken.
10. When the milk starts to thicken, take the saucepan off the flame, and add cream cheese. Mix the cream cheese and make a smooth mixture.
11. In a heat-resistant bowl, add the cheese.
12. Pour this mixture over the cheese and mix well.
13. Now turn on the grill at medium heat level.
14. Now take an aluminium tray and spread the cooked macaroni in its base.
15. Pour the cream and cheese mixture over the macaroni such that it is fully immersed in the mixture.
16. Put the aluminium tray on the grill and close the hood.
17. Let it stay for 1 hour and then take out.
18. Let it rest for a few minutes.
19. Enjoy your mac and cheese separately or with barbequed chicken or meat.

GRILLED HONEY BEEF

Serves 5

Ingredients
- 1 ½ kg round beef steak
- ¼ cup honey
- ¼ cup soy sauce
- ¼ cup Worcestershire sauce
- ¼ cup brown sugar
- 2 tsp garlic powder
- 1 tbsp red pepper flakes
- 1 tsp salt
- 2 tsp onion powder

Instructions
1. First, prepare the beef by trimming the extra fat and skin from the meat.
2. Next, cut the meat into ¼ inch slices.
3. Make sure that the slices are evenly cut.
4. Set the meat aside.
5. In a medium-size saucepan, add the honey, soy sauce, Worcestershire sauce, pepper, salt, garlic powder, onion powder, and sugar.
6. Simmer it over the flame until a uniform mixture is formed.
7. Let the mixture reach room temperature.
8. Apply the mixture generously on the beef slices and put them in a zip lock bag.
9. Pour the remaining sauce into the zip lock bag.
10. Let it in the refrigerator overnight.
11. The next day, prepare the grill and turn it on with the maximum heat setting.
12. Meanwhile, please take out the beef slices and set them on a tray, and let them reach room temperature.
13. After that, arrange them in an aluminium tray and put them on the grill.
14. Close the grill hood and let it grill for 3 hours.
15. Take it out after three hours and rest for about 2 to 3 hours until it becomes dry.
16. You can consume it as a snack and store it in an airtight container for up to 2 weeks.

GRILLED STRIPED BASS

Serves 6

Ingredients

- 1 kg striped sea bass fillets
- ¼ cup brown sugar
- 4 cups water
- ¼ cup salt
- 2 bay leaves.
- 2 tsp black pepper
- 5 to 6 lemon slices
- ½ cup dry wine
- 3 tsp olive oil

Instructions

1. Clean and wash the fish fillets.
2. Heat the four cups of water and dissolve salt and sugar in them.
3. Let it come to room temperature.
4. When it is at room temperature add, bay leaves, pepper, wine, and lemon slices.
5. Put in the fish fillets inside this brine such that they are completely soaked.
6. Cover them and leave them overnight.
7. The next day turn on the grill at medium heat settings.
8. Bring out the fish fillets and take them out of the brine and wash them with cold water.
9. Set them on the counter on a tray lined with paper towels.
10. Let them dry and come to room temperature.
11. Meanwhile, coat the grills with olive oil.
12. When the fish fillets have reached room temperature, set them on the grill for 5 minutes on each side.
13. Please take off the fish from the grill and let it rest for 10 minutes before serving.

GRILLED CAJUN JUMBO SHRIMPS

Serves 6

Ingredients
- 1 kg jumbo shrimps
- ¼ cup salt
- 2 tbsp dried thyme
- 3 tbsp paprika
- 2 tsp cayenne pepper
- 2 tbsp onion powder
- 3 tbsp black pepper
- 2 tbsp garlic powder
- 3 tbsp olive oil
- ¼ cup lemon juice
- 1 bunch fresh parsley

Instructions
1. Prepare the shrimps.
2. Take out the shells and devein them.
3. Wash and pat them dry.
4. In a bowl, prepare the dry rum.
5. Add salt, sugar, cayenne pepper, paprika, garlic powder, thyme, and onion powder.
6. Mix this carefully.
7. Next, prepare an aluminium tray by greasing it with olive oil.
8. Place the shrimps on the tray in a single layer.
9. Apply the dry rum to the shrimps generously.
10. Let the grill preheat for 20 minutes.
11. Meanwhile, pour lemon juice over the shrimps.
12. Put the shrimps on the grill and close the hood.
13. Please take out the shrimps after 30 minutes or as soon as they start turning pink.
14. This dish can be served warmed or even at room temperature.

GRILLED SCALLOPS WITH VINAIGRETTE

Serves 5

Ingredients
- 1 kg sea scallops
- 3 tbsp olive oil
- 1 tsp salt
- 2 garlic cloves minced.
- 1 tsp pepper

Instructions
1. Wash the scallops under cold running water and dry them on a paper towel.
2. In a bowl, mix the oil, salt, pepper, and lemon juice.
3. Apply the mixture to the scallops.
4. Turn on the grill for medium to high heat setting.
5. Meanwhile, lightly grease an aluminium pan and place the scallops on it such that the scallops do not touch each other.
6. Put the scallops on the grill and cover with the grill hood.
7. Let the scallops in the grill for 40 minutes, and then let them off the grill.
8. Let the scallops rest for 10 minutes and then serve with a fresh green salad and a vinaigrette.

GRILLED CHICKEN WINGS

Serves 4

Ingredients
- 2.5 kg chicken wings
- 2 tsp salt
- 1 tsp pepper
- 1 tsp onion powder
- 1 tsp garlic powder
- ¼ cup paprika
- 1 tsp cayenne pepper
- ½ cup brown sugar

Instructions
1. Wash the chicken wings with cold water and trim them.
2. If you wish, you can break the wings in half or keep them full.
3. Depends on your preference.
4. Next, mix the paprika, salt, pepper, onion powder, garlic powder, sugar, and cayenne pepper in a big mixing bowl.
5. Toss the chicken wings into this spice rub.
6. Use your hands to coat the chicken wings with the spice rub.
7. Heat the grill and put the chicken wings on the grill.
8. Grill the wings for 7 to 8 minutes on each side and then take them off the grill in a platter.
9. Serve the delicious chicken wings immediately.

FRESH HERBAL CHICKEN

Serves 4

Ingredients
- 2.5 kg chicken wings
- 2.5 kg ½ cup olive oil
- 2 garlic minced.
- 2 tbsp rosemary leaves
- 2 tbsp fresh basil leaves
- 2 tbsp lemon juice
- 1 ½ tsp salt
- 1 tsp pepper
- 2 tbsp oregano

Instructions
1. Prepare the chicken wings by trimming them.
2. Wash the wings under cold running water.
3. It is your choice to break the wings into half or use them as it is.
4. In a large mixing bowl, add all ingredients and herbs and make a smooth mixture.
5. Save half and toss the chicken wings in the other half.
6. Use your hands to toss the wings in the mixture so that it is evenly applied.
7. Preheat the grill.
8. Arrange the chicken wings on the grill.
9. Grill for 7 minutes on each side.
10. Check for doneness.
11. The meat on the wings should be tender.
12. Take off the wings from the grill.
13. Let them rest for 5 to 10 minutes before serving.

GRILLED REDFISH FILLETS

Serves 6

Ingredients
- 2 redfish fillets with skin
- 600g ½ cup salt
- 1 tsp black pepper
- 1 tsp lemon zest
- 1 tsp garlic powder
- 1tsp 2 slices of lemon

Instructions
1. Wash the fish fillets with cold running water.
2. Next, prepare a rub by mixing all the ingredients and spices.
3. Apply the rub on the fish fillets generously.
4. Wrap the fish fillets in cling film and refrigerate them overnight.
5. The next day takes out the fish fillets and brings them to room temperature.
6. Prepare the grill.
7. Preheat it to a medium heat level.
8. When the fillets are at room temperature, wash them and pat them dry.
9. Put them in aluminium foil and place them on the grill.
10. Frill for 1 hour and keep flipping the fish occasionally.
11. After 1 hour, take the fish off the grill and then unwrap the foil.
12. Let the fillets rest for 30 minutes before serving.

GRILLED GINGER DORY

Serves 4

Ingredients
- 4 fillets of dory
- 1 tsp onion Powder
- ½ cup salt
- 2 tsp black pepper
- 1 tsp ginger powder
- 1 tsp garlic powder
- Coriander for garnish
- Lemon slices for garnish

Instructions
1. Wash the fish fillets with cold running water.
2. Next, prepare a rub by mixing all the ingredients and spices.
3. Apply the rub on the fish fillets generously.
4. Wrap the fish fillets in cling film and refrigerate them overnight.
5. The next day takes out the fish fillets and brings them to room temperature.
6. Prepare the electric Smoker with wood chips and water.
7. Turn it on at 220°F.
8. When the fillets are at room temperature, wash them and pat them dry.
9. Preheat the grill.
10. Grill the fish fillets for 4 minutes on each side.
11. Let the fillets rest for 30 minutes before serving.
12. Garnish the fish fillets with coriander and lemon slices for serving.

GRILLED HERBAL SALMON FILLETS

Serves 4

Ingredients
- 750 g Salmon fillets
- ¼ cup salt
- ¼ cup sugar
- ½ cup water
- 2 tbsp black pepper
- 2 slices lemon
- 1 bunch fresh dill

Instructions
1. Prepare the marinade for the fish.
2. In a flat dish, pour water, salt, sugar, and pepper.
3. Mix them well. Soak the fish fillets in the marinade and cover them with dill and lemon slices.
4. Wrap the fillets in cling wrap and refrigerate overnight.
5. The next day, take out the fish fillets, remove the cling wrap, and bring them to room temperature.
6. Preheat the grill.
7. Grill the fish fillets for 4 minutes on each side.
8. Take off from the grill and let it rest for 5 minutes before serving.

GRILLED PAPRIKA CHICKEN

Serves 4

Ingredients
- 1 kg chicken breast pieces
- 2 tsp black pepper
- 2 tsp salt
- 4 tbsp lemon juice
- 2 tbsp paprika

Instructions
1. Wash the chicken breast pieces.
2. It is your choice to remove the skin or keep it.
3. Pat the chicken dry.
4. In a flat dish, mix the salt, pepper, paprika, and lemon juice.
5. Apply the mixture generously on the chicken and wrap the pieces with cling wrap and leave it in the refrigerator overnight.
6. The next day, take out the chicken from the fridge and let it warm up to room temperature.
7. Wash the chicken fillets under cold water.
8. Pat, the chicken, dries with paper towels.
9. Now, preheat the grill.
10. Grill the chicken fillets on the grill.
11. Grill the chicken for 7 minutes on each side.
12. Take the chicken from the grill and serve with your choice of sides.

SOY SAUCE WITH GRILLED SALMON

Serves 4

Ingredients
- 300g salmon
- ¼ cup maple syrup
- ¼ teaspoon pepper
- 2 ½ tablespoon soy sauce
- 2 clove garlic chopped
- ½ teaspoon garlic powder

Instructions
1. Preheat the grill.
2. Mix the garlic, soy sauce, maple syrup, garlic salt, and pepper in a small bowl.
3. Put the fish in an oven-safe glass dish and pour the maple mixture on it.
4. Rub the mixture on the fish so that it is fully coated.
5. Put a cling wrap on the dish and marinate the fish for 20 minutes in the fridge.
6. After 20 minutes, turn the fish and cover it again.
7. Let it marinate for 20 more minutes.
8. Take out the baking dish from the fridge and take off cling wrap.
9. Now wrap the fish in aluminium foil.
10. Put the fish on the grill and cover the grill with the cover.
11. Grill the fish for 50 minutes and keep flipping them occasionally.
12. Remove the aluminium foil and put it on the serving plate.
13. Check for doneness with a fork.
14. If a fork easily flakes the fish, it means it is done.

GRILLED OKRA

Serves 4

Ingredients
- 500g okra
- ½ teaspoon garlic powder
- ¼ teaspoon ground black pepper
- 2 teaspoon olive oil
- ½ cup cornmeal
- ½ cup breadcrumbs

Instructions
1. Preheat the grill on a low to medium heat setting.
2. Prepare a tray.
3. Wash okra and pat dry.
4. Spread on the tray in a single layer.
5. The drying is critical.
6. If any moisture is left, the okra can taste soggy rather than crunchy.
7. Slit the okra in the centre without fully cutting it.
8. In a large bowl, add garlic powder, pepper, cornmeal, breadcrumbs, and pepper.
9. Fill this breadcrumb filling in the slit okra.
10. Brush the okra with olive oil.
11. Grill the vegetable for 5 to 7 minutes with flipping and turning occasionally.
12. Take off from the grill and serve immediately while it is crunchy.

GRILLED TUNA AND BROCCOLI PASTA SEAFOOD

Serves 6-8

Ingredients
- 400g tuna fish fillets
- 500g macaroni
- 250g broccoli chopped
- 2 tablespoon flour
- 3 slices sourdough bread
- 500ml milk
- 2 red onions, finely chopped
- 4 tablespoon vinegar
- 50g butter
- 2 tablespoon mustard
- 250g cheddar cheese
- 2 tablespoon capers
- 3 tablespoon chopped parsley

Instructions
1. Heat the grill at medium heat level.
2. Wash the tuna fillets and rub some olive oil on them.
3. Season with salt and freshly ground pepper.
4. Grill the tuna on the grill for 4 to 7 minutes on each side.
5. Take care that the fish is not burnt.
6. Set aside on a cutting board.
7. Cut into thick slices and set aside.
8. Meanwhile, preheat the oven at 300°F.
9. Mix onion and vinegar in a small bowl. Set aside.
10. Cook pasta for 8 minutes in boiling water.
11. Drain the water and set pasta aside.
12. Put broccoli in a steamer and steam for five minutes.
13. Prepare the white sauce.
14. Take a large saucepan, melt the butter.
15. Add the flour slowly and mix.
16. No lumps should be formed.
17. Cook for at least two minutes.
18. Turn off the heat and add milk gradually and mix well.

19. Take care that no lumps are formed.
20. Turn on the heat and cook on a high flame for two minutes.
21. Turn off the heat and add the mustard and cheese and mix till the cheese melts.
22. To this sauce, add the pasta and broccoli and half of the parsley.
23. Drain the vinegar from the onion and add the onion to the white sauce.
24. Put all of this in a large oven-safe dish.
25. Scatter some sourdough pieces on the top of the dish.
26. Bake for 30 minutes.
27. The dish will be bubbly after taking out of the oven.
28. Wait for it to stop bubbling.
29. Serve the pasta with grilled tuna on the side.
30. Serve immediately

GRILLED GARLIC CHICKEN

Serves 4

Ingredients
- 1kg chicken thighs
- 1 tablespoon olive oil
- 2 tablespoons honey
- 2 tablespoon garlic paste
- 3 tablespoons honey
- 1 teaspoon cayenne pepper
- Salt to taste

Instructions
1. Preheat the grill to a high heat setting.
2. Wash and clean chicken drumsticks.
3. Dry them with a paper towel.
4. Make diagonal cuts on the chicken meat.
5. Two cuts on each drumstick.
6. This will make sure that the marinade will impart flavour throughout the chicken.
7. Put chicken thighs in a baking pan.
8. Rub olive oil on the chicken.
9. Next, rub garlic paste on the chicken.
10. Rub some into the slits as well.
11. Mix salt and cayenne pepper with honey and pour over the chicken.
12. Rub the honey pic on the chicken and to the slits as well.
13. Cover the chicken with aluminium foil and grill for 20 minutes.
14. Keep flipping occasionally so that the heat is evenly distributed.
15. Take out the chicken, remove the aluminium foil, and again grill for about 4 minutes on each side so that grill marks can be formed and the chicken is thoroughly cooked.
16. Serve hot.

GRILLED COD FISH FILLETS

Serves 1-2

Ingredients

- 2 cod fish fillets
- 2 tablespoon lemon juice
- 2 tablespoons oil
- 1 tablespoon chopped parsley
- 2 tablespoon lemon juice
- ½ teaspoon cayenne pepper
- Salt to taste

Instructions

1. First, preheat the grill for a medium heat setting.
2. Rinse the fish fillets with cold water and pat dry with a paper towel.
3. Put all the fish fillets on a dish.
4. In a small bowl, add lemon juice, salt, and cayenne pepper.
5. Pour this over the fish and rub a little.
6. Grill the fish fillets for 4 minutes on each side and take them out on a serving platter.
7. Check for doneness.
8. Use a fork to check if the fish easily flakes.
9. It means it is done.
10. Top with fresh parsley.
11. Serve hot.

PARMESAN CHEESE WITH GRILLED TILAPIA FISH FILLET

Serves 4

Ingredients
- 4 fillets (medium size) of tilapia fish
- 3 cloves garlic chopped
- ½ cup Parmesan cheese
- 2 tablespoon chopped parsley
- 2 tablespoons freshly squeezed lemon juice
- 2 tablespoons olive oil
- 1 lemon cut in wedges
- ½ teaspoon cayenne pepper
- ½ teaspoon pepper salt to taste

Instructions
1. First, preheat the grill at a medium heat setting.
2. Wash the fish fillets water and dry with a paper towel.
3. Put all the fish fillets in the baking dish.
4. In a small bowl, mix garlic, cayenne pepper, salt, olive oil, black pepper, and lemon juice.
5. Pour this over the fish fillets.
6. Now grill the fish fillets on the grill.
7. Fish usually takes less time to grill.
8. Grill each side for 3 to 4 minutes and then take off from the grill into a serving platter.
9. Top the fish fillets with parmesan cheese and fresh parsley.
10. Serve hot with fresh lemon slices.

GRILLED PEPPER BEEF

Serves 12

Ingredients
- 3kg beef
- 2 tablespoon coarse pepper
- ¾ cup horseradish grated
- 2 tablespoon sugar
- Salt to taste.

Instructions
1. Obtain a large piece of beef meat without the bone.
2. Tie it to form a loaf shape.
3. In a small bowl, mix salt and sugar.
4. Rub the beef with this mixture.
5. Line a deep baking dish with aluminium foil and place the beef on it.
6. Cover with cling wrap and chill for 3 hours in the fridge.
7. Take out the beef after three hours.
8. Remove the cling wrap.
9. In a small bowl, mix salt, pepper, and horseradish.
10. Pat horseradish mixture over the top and sides of beef.
11. Heat up the grill.
12. Cover the beef with aluminium foil completely and place it on the grill.
13. Cover it with the grill cover.
14. Let it grill for 1 hour and 30 minutes, flipping it occasionally.
15. Take out from the grill and remove the aluminium foil.
16. Let it rest for 10 minutes.
17. Next, cut into thin slices.
18. Save the juices released while grilling and pour over the meat slices for flavour.
19. Serve warm.
20. Enjoy your meal.

GRILLED BEEF TERIYAKI

Serves 2-4

Ingredients
- 1 ½ kg beef steak
- 2 tablespoon garlic (chopped)
- 1 cup potato (diced)
- 1 cup store-bought teriyaki marinade
- 1 onion sliced
- 1 carrot sliced
- 2 tablespoon olive oil.
- ½ teaspoon black pepper

Instructions
1. Cut the beef into strips.
2. Remove as much fat as possible.
3. Rub the beef with garlic.
4. In a large bowl, mix the potatoes, carrots, onions, and beef.
5. Pour the teriyaki marinade and olive oil.
6. Coat all the ingredients with marinade.
7. Leave to marinate for 4 hours.
8. Heat up the grill to maximum heat level.
9. Meanwhile, prepare an aluminium dish.
10. Put all the beef and marinade in the dish and cover it with aluminium foil.
11. By covering it with aluminium foil.
12. Put the dish on the grill and cover it with the grill cover.
13. Let it grill for 45 mins to 1 hour.
14. Check if the beef is tender.
15. Serve warm.

GRILLED CHICKEN TERIYAKI

Serves 2-4

Ingredients
- 1 ½ kg chicken steak
- 2 tablespoon garlic (chopped)
- 1 cup potato (diced)
- 1 cup store-bought teriyaki marinade
- 1 onion sliced
- 1 carrot sliced
- 2 tablespoon olive oil.
- ½ teaspoon black pepper

Instructions
1. Cut the chicken into strips.
2. Remove as much fat as possible.
3. Rub the chicken with garlic.
4. In a large bowl, mix the potatoes, carrots, onions, and beef.
5. Pour the teriyaki marinade and olive oil.
6. Coat all the ingredients with marinade.
7. Leave to marinate for 4 hours.
8. Preheat the grill for a high heat setting.
9. Meanwhile, prepare the aluminium dish and put all the beef and marinade in the dish.
10. Cover it with aluminium foil.
11. Put the dish on the grill and cover it with a grill cover.
12. Grill for 45 minutes.
13. After 45 minutes, check if the chicken is tender.
14. Serve warm.

RICE VINEGAR WITH GRILLED SEABASS

Serves 2-3

Ingredients
- 750g sea bass
- ¾ tablespoon sesame oil
- 2 clove garlic sliced
- 2 green onions
- 2 tablespoon ginger slices
- 1 ½ soy sauce
- ½ tbsp rice vinegar

Instructions
1. First, heat up the grill for a medium to high heat setting.
2. Snip the corners of the spring onions and peel off the rough outer layer (both dark green and stem).
3. Break them into 5-7 cm (approximately 2-3 inch) bits and cut them by the length in half.
4. Slice the ginger into thin strips and peel and chop the garlic into small pieces.
5. Cover a baking dish wide enough to accommodate the fish with a sheet of aluminium foil that is large enough to fold the fish together with a little extra.
6. Spread a layer of onion, ginger, and garlic at the bottom of the foil.
7. Create two cuts on each side of the sea bass, then put them on top of the onion, garlic, and ginger slices.
8. Place in the dish a few more bits of onion, ginger, and garlic, then place the few slices of garlic and ginger into the slits on the side of the fish.
9. One onion should still be remaining.
10. Combine the soya sauce, rice vinegar, and sesame oil and spread over the fish.
11. To close up the package, wrap the fish into the foil and secure it on the edges by folding.
12. Grill the fish while wrapped in the aluminium foil.
13. Turn it and flip it after every 5 to 6 minutes.
14. Grill for 20 minutes.
15. Check for doneness.
16. The fish should be thoroughly done.
17. Serve hot, topped with the remaining onion.

GRILLED CHICKEN AND LETTUCE WRAP

Serves 1

Ingredients
- 2 whole iceberg lettuce leaves
- 100g chicken cubed.
- 1 tbsp olive oil
- 1 tbsp mustard
- 2 tsp lemon juice
- 15 g chopped cilantro
- 25 g chopped green onion
- 1 garlic clove minced
- 1 small carrot chopped
- 1 tsp chili flakes

Instructions
1. Chill the lettuce leaves in the freezer for 10 minutes.
2. Meanwhile, cook the chicken cubes in 1 tbsp oil for 10-15 mins on low flame.
3. Put the cooked chicken in a bowl, mix all the remaining ingredients except for the lettuce leaves.
4. On a plate, set the lettuce leaves side by side and spoon the mixture onto the leaves.
5. Wrap the lettuce leaves.
6. Heat up the grill and grill the lettuce wraps for 2 to 3 minutes.
7. Enjoy your grilled lettuce wraps.

FISH TACOS

Serves 1

Ingredients

- 100 g boneless fish
- 1 small onion sliced.
- 3 tbsp ranch
- 1 small tomato sliced.
- 100 g lettuce chopped.
- 2 soft shell tacos
- ½ tsp salt
- ½ tsp pepper
- 2 tbsp oil to fry
- 100 g grated cheese

Instructions

1. In a frying pan, fry fish in oil and add salt and pepper.
2. Cook for 5 minutes and then take out on a plate.
3. Now assemble the tocos by adding lettuce, fish, then tomatoes and onions.
4. Top with grated cheese and fold the taco.
5. Brush olive oil lightly on the outer side of the tacos.
6. Heat up the grill and grill the tocos for 2 minutes on each side.
7. You will get warm toasty tacos with melted cheese.
8. Enjoy your meal.

CHICKEN TACOS

Serves 1

Ingredients
- 100 g boneless chicken breast
- 1 small onion sliced.
- 2 tbsp ranch
- 1 small tomato sliced.
- 100 g lettuce chopped.
- 2 soft shell tacos
- ½ tbsp salt
- ½ tbsp pepper
- 3 tbsp oil to fry
- 100 g grated cheese

Instructions
1. Cut the chicken breast into small pieces.
2. In a frying pan, fry chicken in oil and add salt and pepper.
3. Cook for 10 minutes and then take out on a plate.
4. Now assemble the tacos by putting, lettuce, chicken, then tomatoes and onions.
5. Top with grated cheese and fold the taco.
6. Brush a little bit of olive oil on the tacos.
7. Heat up the grill and grill the tacos for 2 minutes on each side.
8. Serve the tacos warm and toasty.
9. Enjoy your meal.

PRAWN TACOS

Serves 2

Ingredients

- 100 g prawns
- 1 small onion sliced.
- 3 tbsp ranch
- 1 small tomato sliced.
- 100 g lettuce chopped.
- 2 soft shell tacos
- ½ tsp salt
- ½ tsp pepper
- 3 tbsp oil to fry
- 100 g grated cheese

Instructions

1. Peel the skin off the prawns and devein them.
2. Wash them with cold water.
3. In a frying pan, fry prawns in oil and add salt and pepper.
4. Cook for 3 minutes and then take out on a plate.
5. Now assemble the tocos by putting, lettuce, prawns, then tomatoes and onions.
6. Top with grated cheese and fold the taco.
7. Heat the grill and grill the tacos on the heated grill.
8. Grill for 2 minutes on both sides.
9. Serve when warm and toasty.

GRILLED CHICKEN WITH RICE

Serves 2

Ingredients
- 200 g chicken breast
- 2 tbsp ginger thinly sliced.
- 5 green chilis sliced longitudinally.
- ½ tsp salt
- ½ tsp pepper 2tbsp vinegar
- 2 tbsp soy sauce
- 1 tbsp chili sauce
- 2 tbsp olive oil

Instructions
1. Preheat the grill for medium to high heat setting.
2. Rub the chicken with olive oil and season with salt.
3. Grill the chicken breast.
4. It does not take very long to grill chicken.
5. Grill chicken for 5 minutes on each side and let it rest before slicing.
6. After 5 minutes, slice the chicken into thin strips.
7. In a mixing bowl, add chicken with vinegar, soy sauce, chili sauce, salt, and pepper.
8. Put this mixture in a pan and flame for 2 minutes and take it out on a plate.
9. Garnish with ginger and green chili.
10. Serve warm with boiled rice.

CURRY CHICKEN BURGERS

Serves 2

Ingredients
- 100 g chicken mince
- ½ tsp salt
- ½ tsp curry powder
- 2 tbsp chopped coriander
- 2 tbsp chopped onion
- 2 tbsp chopped tomato
- 1 tsp oil
- 2 burger buns

Instructions
1. In a large mixing bowl, add the chicken mince.
2. Mix all the ingredients except the oil.
3. Mix well.
4. Now make two thick burger patties.
5. Coat the patties with olive oil.
6. Heat up the grill and put the burger patties on the grill.
7. It does not take long for chicken patties to cook.
8. Grill for 4 minutes on each side and then take off from the grill.
9. Set them in the burger bun and enjoy with tomato ketchup.

CHICKEN MINCE BUNS

Serves 2

Ingredients
- 100 g chicken mince
- ½ tsp salt
- ½ tsp curry powder
- 2 tbsp chopped coriander
- 2 tbsp chopped onion
- 2 tbsp chopped tomato
- Oil to fry
- 2 burger buns

Instructions
1. In a large mixing bowl, add the chicken mince.
2. Mix all the ingredients except the oil.
3. Mix well.
4. Now make two thick burger patties.
5. Grill the burger patties.
6. Beef usually takes longer.
7. It will take around 7 to 8 minutes on each side.
8. Be sure that the patties are fully cooked and then take off from the grill.
9. Arrange them in the burger bun and enjoy with tomato ketchup.

TASTY SALAD

COUSCOUS TABBOULEH SALAD

Serves 4

Ingredients
- 1 cup couscous
- 1 cup boiling water
- ½ cucumber, diced
- 1 tomato, diced
- 4 tablespoons sunflower seeds
- 1 cup fresh parsley, chopped
- 2 scallions, chopped
- ¼ cup chopped fresh mint Zest and juice of 1 lemon 1 garlic clove, pressed
- 1 tablespoon avocado oil (optional)
- Pinch sea salt (optional)

Instructions
1. Pour the couscous in a large bowl, then pour the boiling water over and cover the bowl.
2. Let it sit for 5 minutes or until the couscous is tender.
3. Drain the couscous and add the remaining ingredients.
4. Toss to combine well.
5. Serve.

CHICKPEA AND HEART OF PALM SALAD

Serves 4

Ingredients

- 1 (15½-ounce / 439-g) can chickpeas, drained and rinsed
- 1 (14-ounce / 397-g) can hearts of palm, drained and chopped
- ½ cup diced celery
- ½ cup chopped white onion
- ¼ cup almond butter
- ½ teaspoon sea salt (optional)
- ¼ teaspoon freshly ground black pepper

Instructions

1. Place the chickpeas in a large bowl and mash them into a chunky paste with a hand masher.
2. Make the salad: Add the remaining ingredients to the bowl and toss to combine well.
3. Divide the salad among 4 bowls
4. Serve immediately.

WHITE BEAN AND CARROT SALAD

Serves 2

Ingredients
- 2 tablespoons balsamic vinegar
- 1 tablespoon olive oil (optional)
- 1 tablespoon fresh rosemary, chopped
- 1 tablespoon fresh oregano, chopped
- 1 teaspoon minced fresh chives
- 1 garlic clove, minced Pinch sea salt (optional)

Instructions
1. Salad: 1 (14-ounce / 397-g) can cannellini beans, drained and rinsed 2 carrots, diced 6 mushrooms, thinly sliced 1 zucchini, diced 2 tablespoons fresh basil, chopped
2. In a large bowl, stir together all the ingredients for the dressing.
3. Add all the ingredients for the salad to the bowl and toss to combine well.
4. Divide the salad between 2 bowls.
5. Serve immediately.

CHICKPEA SPINACH SALAD

Serves 1

Ingredients

- 3 cups baby spinach, roughly chopped
- 2 cups cooked chickpeas (drained and rinsed, if canned)
- 1 cup chopped mushrooms
- 1 tomato, chopped
- 1 avocado, peeled, pitted, and chopped
- ⅛ teaspoon pink Himalayan salt
- ⅛ teaspoon freshly ground black pepper Juice of 1 large lemon
- 1 tablespoon sunflower seeds, for topping (optional)
- 1 teaspoon hulled hemp seeds, for topping (optional)

Instructions

1. In a large bowl, combine the spinach, chickpeas, mushrooms, tomato, and avocado.
2. Add the salt, pepper, and lemon juice.
3. Mix thoroughly so all the flavors combine and the avocado is mixed in well.
4. Top with the seeds.
5. Enjoy immediately or store in a reusable container in the refrigerator for up to 5 days.

BARLEY AND STRAWBERRY SALAD

Serves 4

Ingredients
- ¼ cup orange juice
- 2 tablespoons fresh lime juice
- 1 tablespoon olive oil (optional)
- ¼ teaspoon sea salt, plus more to taste (optional)
- ⅛ teaspoon black pepper, plus more to taste
- ½ small red onion, sliced
- 2 cups cooked barley, cooled
- 2 cups strawberries, hulled and chopped
- 1½ cups cooked cannellini beans
- ½ cup chopped cilantro
- 5 ounces (142 g)

Instructions
1. Mixed baby greens ½ cup roasted pistachios, shelled and chopped ½ avocado, diced 1 teaspoon balsamic vinegar
2. In a large bowl, combine the orange juice, lime juice, olive oil (if desired), ¼ teaspoon sea salt (if desired) and ⅛ teaspoon pepper.
3. Make the salad: Add the onion slices, barley, strawberries, cannellini beans, cilantro and mixed baby greens to the bowl. Toss until well blended. Sprinkle with sea salt (if desired) and pepper to taste.
4. Divide the salad into bowls.
5. Spread the roasted pistachios and avocado on top and drizzle with the balsamic vinegar.
6. Serve immediately.

SPRING PENNE SALAD

Serves 4

Ingredients
- 8 cups water
- ½ pound (227 g) asparagus, trimmed and cut into
- ½-inch pieces
- ½ pound (227 g) sugar snap peas, trimmed
- 12 ounces (340 g) whole-grain penne, cooked, drained, and rinsed until cool
- 1 (15-ounce / 425-g) can artichoke hearts (oil-free), drained and quartered
- 4 green onions, white and green parts, thinly sliced
- ¼ cup finely chopped chives
- 1 tablespoon Dijon mustard
- ¼ cup plus
- 2 tablespoons balsamic vinegar
- Salt and freshly ground black pepper, to taste (optional)

Instructions
1. Prepare an ice bath by filling a large bowl with ice and cold water.
2. Bring the water to a boil in a pot and add the asparagus and sugar snap peas, and cook for 3 minutes, then drain and plunge them into the ice bath.
3. Drain the vegetables and combine them with the cooked pasta, artichoke hearts, green onions, and chives.
4. Set aside. In a small bowl, combine the balsamic Dijon mustard, vinegar, and salt (if desired) and pepper.
5. Pour the dressing over the pasta mixture and toss well before serving warm.

INDONESIA GREEN NOODLE SALAD

Serves 4

Ingredients

- 12 ounces (340 g) brown rice noodles, cooked, drained, and rinsed until cool
- 1 cup snow peas, trimmed and sliced in half on the diagonal
- 2 medium cucumbers, peeled, halved, deseeded, and sliced thinly
- 2 heads baby bok choy, trimmed and thinly sliced
- 4 green onions, green and white parts, trimmed and thinly sliced
- 3 tablespoons sambal oelek
- ½ cup chopped cilantro
- 2 tablespoons soy sauce
- ¼ cup fresh lime juice
- ¼ cup finely chopped mint

Instructions

1. Combine all the ingredients in a large bowl and toss to coat well.
2. Serve immediately.

MEDITERRANEAN COUSCOUS SALAD

Serves 1

Ingredients
- 1½ cups water
- 1 cup couscous
- ½ cup cooked chickpeas (drained and rinsed, if canned)
- ½ small red bell pepper, chopped
- 1 small red onion, diced
- ½ cucumber, chopped
- 1 small tomato, chopped
- 1 scallion, chopped
- 1 tablespoon balsamic vinegar
- ⅛ teaspoon pink Himalayan salt
- ⅛ teaspoon freshly ground black pepper

Instructions
1. In a nonstick pot over medium-high heat, bring the water to a boil.
2. Add the couscous.
3. Turn off the heat, stir the couscous, and cover.
4. Let it sit for 5 minutes, until the couscous has fully absorbed the water and is soft.
5. Transfer the couscous to a bowl.
6. Add the chickpeas, bell pepper, onion, cucumber, tomato, scallion, vinegar, salt, and black pepper. Mix well.
7. Serve.

CORN AND TOMATO PASTA SALAD

Serves 4 to 6

Ingredients
- 8 ounces (227 g) pasta
- 1¼ cups frozen corn, thawed
- ¾ cup coconut butter Juice of 1 medium lime
- ½ tablespoon taco seasoning
- 1½ cups cherry tomatoes, sliced
- 1¼ cups black beans, rinsed well
- ¼ cup red onion, finely diced
- 2 tablespoons cilantro stems, finely chopped

Instructions
1. Bring a large pot of water to boil over medium heat.
2. Add the pasta to the pot and cook for 10 to 15 minutes, or until just softened.
3. Drain the pasta and rinse the pasta with cold water to bring it down to room temperature.
4. In a large mixing bowl, whisk together the coconut butter, lime juice and taco seasoning.
5. Add the cooled pasta, thawed corn, cherry tomatoes, black beans, onion and cilantro stems to the bowl.
6. Toss to combine well.
7. Divide the pasta salad among serving bowls and serve immediately.

KIDNEY BEAN AND TOMATO CHILI

Serves 4 bowls

Ingredients

- 2 to 3 garlic cloves, minced
- 1 onion, diced
- 1 to 2 tablespoons water, vegetable broth, or red wine
- ¼ cup tomato paste or crushed tomatoes
- 1 (28-ounce / 794-g) can tomatoes
- 2 to 3 teaspoons chili powder
- 1 (14-ounce / 397-g) can kidney beans, rinsed and drained, or 1½ cups cooked
- ¼ teaspoon sea salt (optional)
- ¼ cup fresh cilantro or parsley leaves

Instructions

1. Add the garlic, onion, and water in a large pot and sauté for about 5 minutes until the vegetables are softened.
2. Mix in the tomato paste, tomatoes, chili powder, and beans.
3. Sprinkle with the salt, if desired.
4. Bring the mixture to a simmer for at least 10 minutes, or until cooked to your preferred doneness, stirring occasionally.
5. Divide the chili among bowls and serve garnished with cilantro.

MEDITBLACK BEAN PASTA SALAD

Serves 4

Ingredients
- 8 ounces (227 g) whole wheat rotini pasta
- 1 large avocado, halved and pitted
- 2 tablespoons freshly squeezed lime juice
- 1½ teaspoons chili powder
- 1 teaspoon smoked paprika
- 1 teaspoon ground cumin
- 1 garlic clove, chopped
- 1 (15-ounce /425-g) can corn, drained
- 1 (15-ounce /425-g) black beans, drained and rinsed
- 1 small red bell pepper, diced
- 1 pint cherry tomatoes, halved
- ¼ cup chopped red onion
- ½ cup chopped fresh cilantro

Instructions
1. Cook the pasta according to package instructions.
2. Drain, rinse lightly, and let cool.
3. Scoop the avocado flesh into a blender and add the lime juice, chili powder, paprika, cumin, and garlic.
4. Blend until smooth. In a large bowl, toss together the pasta, corn, black beans, bell pepper, tomatoes, red onion, cilantro, and dressing until well mixed.
5. Refrigerate for at least 1 hour before serving or, for best results, up to 1 day.

DIJON POTATO SALAD

Serves 4

Ingredients

- 5 large red or golden potatoes, cut into
- 1-inch cubes
- 1 cup silken tofu or 1 large avocado
- ¼ cup chopped fresh chives
- 2 tablespoons
- Dijon mustard
- ½ tablespoon freshly squeezed lemon juice
- ½ teaspoon garlic powder
- ½ teaspoon onion powder
- ½ teaspoon dried dill
- ¼ teaspoon freshly ground black pepper

Instructions

1. Bring a large pot of water to a boil over high heat.
2. Immerse the potatoes in the hot water gently and carefully.
3. Boil for 10 minutes, or until the potatoes can be easily pierced with a fork. Drain.
4. Put the potatoes in a large bowl, and refrigerate for a minimum of 20 minutes.
5. Meanwhile, put the tofu in a separate large bowl. Using a fork or mixing spoon, smash the tofu until creamy.
6. Whisk in the chives, mustard, lemon juice, garlic powder, onion powder, dill, and pepper until well combined.
7. Stir the cooled potatoes into the creamy dressing.
8. Mix gently until the potatoes are well coated.
9. Refrigerate the dish for at least 30 minutes or until ready to serve.

SALAD WITH VINAIGRETTE

Serves 4

Ingredients
For the vinaigrette
- ½ cup olive oil 4 tbsps. balsamic vinegar
- 2 tbsps. chopped fresh oregano
- Pinch red pepper flakes
- Ground black pepper

For the salad
- 4 cups shredded green leaf lettuce
- 1 carrot, shredded
- ¾ cup fresh green beans, cut into 1-inch pieces
- 3 large radishes, sliced thin

Instructions
1. To make the vinaigrette: put the vinaigrette ingredients in a bowl and whisk.
2. In a bowl, to make the salad, toss together the carrot, lettuce, green beans, and radishes.
3. Add the vinaigrette to the vegetables and toss to coat.
4. Arrange the salad on plates and serve.

SALAD WITH LEMON DRESSING

Serves 4

Ingredients
- ¼ cup heavy cream
- ¼ cup freshly squeezed lemon juice
- 2 tbsps. granulated sugar
- 2 tbsps. chopped fresh dill
- 2 tbsps. finely chopped scallion, green part only
- ¼ tsp. ground black pepper
- 1 English cucumber, thinly sliced
- 2 cups shredded green cabbage

Instructions
1. In a small bowl, stir together the lemon juice, cream, sugar, dill, scallion, and pepper until well blended.
2. In a large bowl, toss together the cucumber and cabbage.
3. Place the salad in the refrigerator and chill for 1 hour.
4. Stir before serving.

HAWAIIAN CHICKEN SALAD

Serves 4

Ingredients
- 1 ½ cups of chicken breast, cooked, chopped
- 1 cup pineapple chunks
- 1 ¼ cups lettuce iceberg, shredded
- ½ cup celery, diced
- ½ cup mayonnaise
- 1/8 tsp (dash)
- Tabasco sauce
- 2 lemon juice
- ¼ tsp black pepper

Instructions
1. Combine the cooked chicken, pineapple, lettuce, and celery in a medium bowl. Just set aside.
2. In a small bowl, make the dressing. Mix the mayonnaise, Tabasco sauce, pepper, and lemon juice.
3. Use the chicken mixture to add the dressing and stir until well mixed.

GRATED CARROT SALAD WITH LEMON-DIJON VINAIGRETTE

Serves 8

Ingredients
- 9 small carrots (14 cm),peeled
- 2 tbsp. ½ teaspoon Dijon mustard - 1 C. lemon juice
- 2 tbsp. extra virgin olive oil
- 1-2 tsp. honey (to taste)
- ¼ tsp. salt
- ¼ tsp. freshly ground pepper (to taste) - 2 tbsp. chopped parsley
- 1 green onion, thinly sliced

Instructions
1. Grate the carrots in a food processor.
2. In a salad bowl, mix Dijon mustard, lemon juice, honey, olive oil, salt, and pepper. Add the carrots, fresh parsley, and green onions. Stir to coat well. Cover and refrigerate until ready to be served.

TUNA MACARONI SALAD

Serves 10

Ingredients
- 1 ½ cups Uncooked Macaroni
- 1 170 g Can of tuna in water
- ¼ cup Mayonnaise
- 2 medium celery stalks, diced
- 1 Tbsp. Lemon Pepper Seasoning

Instructions
1. Cook the pasta and let it cool in the refrigerator.
2. Drain the tuna in a colander and rinse it with cold water.
3. Add the tuna and celery once the macaroni has cooled.
4. Stir in mayonnaise and sprinkle with lemon seasoning. Mix well.
5. Serve cold.

FRUITY ZUCCHINI SALAD

Serves 4

Ingredients
- 400 g zucchini
- 1 small onion
- 4 tbsp. olive oil
- 100 g pineapple preserve, drained
- Salt, paprika
- Thyme

Instructions
1. Dice the onions and sauté in the oil until translucent.
2. Cut the zucchini into slices and add. Season with salt, paprika, and thyme.
3. Let cool and mix with the cut pineapple.

COUSCOUS SALAD

Serves 5

Ingredients
- 3 cups of water
- ½ tsp. cinnamon tea
- ½ tsp. cumin tea
- 1 tsp. honey soup
- 2 tbsp. lemon juice
- 3 cups quick-cooking couscous
- 2 tbsp. tea of olive oil
- 1 green onion,
- Finely chopped 1 small carrot, finely diced
- ½ red pepper,
- Finely diced fresh coriander

Instructions
1. Stir in the water with the cinnamon, cumin, honey, and lemon juice and bring to a boil. Put the couscous in it, cover it, and remove it from the heat. To swell the couscous, stir with a fork. Add the vegetables, fresh herbs, and olive oil. It is possible to serve the salad warm or cold.

CORN TORTILLAS AND SPINACH SALAD

Serves 1

Ingredients

- 4 corn tortillas
- 2 cups baby spinach
- 2 tbsp red onion (chopped)
- 1 pepper
- 4 mini tomatoes (whole)
- 8 pitted small ripe olives
- 2 tsp balsamic vinegar
- 1/8 tsp salt
- 1/8 tsp pepper
- 1 tbsp extra virgin olive oil

Instructions

1. Heat tortillas according to package instruction.
2. Mix remaining ingredients in a salad bowl.
3. Serve tortillas and salad.
4. I often cook this dish for dinner, my children adore it

COBB SALAD

Serves 1

Ingredients

- 4 Cherry Tomatoes, chopped
- ¼ cup Bacon, cooked & crumbled
- 1/2 of 1 Avocado, chopped
- 2 oz. Chicken Breast, shredded
- 1 Egg, hardboiled
- 2 cups Mixed Green salad
- 1 oz. Feta Cheese, crumbled

Instructions

1. Toss all the ingredients for the Cobb salad in a large mixing bowl and toss well.
2. Serve and enjoy it.

CREAMY BELL PEPPER CORN SALAND AND SEARED ZUCCHINI

Serves 2

Ingredients

- 2 zucchini
- 2 cups corn kernels
- 3 cherry tomatoes (whole)
- 1/2 cup celery
- 1/3 cup green bell pepper
- 2 tbsp sour cream (reduced-fat)
- 1/4 cup mayonnaise (reduced-fat)
- 1/8 tsp pepper
- 1 tsp sugar
- 1/4 tsp salt

Instructions

1. Cook corn (you can find instructions on the package).
2. Mix corn, chopped celery, chopped green bell pepper, whole cherry tomatoes, sour cream, mayonnaise, sugar, 1/8 tsp salt and pepper in a bowl.
3. Heat a large skillet and cook cut in half lengthwise zucchini 8 minutes (turn occasionally).
4. Sprinkle zucchini with 1/8 tsp salt.
5. Add zucchini to the corn mixture.
6. You can serve corn salad and zucchini alongside any meat dish.
7. Creamy Bell Pepper-Corn Salad and Seared Zucchini is a dish for a quick and satisfying family dinner.

CAULIFLOWER AND SPINACH SALAD

Serves 1

Ingredients

- 1/2 (12-oz) pkg cauliflower florets
- 1 (5-oz) pkg spinach
- 1 (8.25-oz) can mandarin oranges (drained)
- 1/4 cup almonds
- 1 tbsp extra virgin olive oil
- 1 tbsp apple vinegar
- 2 tsp honey
- 1/8 tsp salt

Instructions

1. Cook cauliflower.
2. Mix vinegar, oil, honey, and salt; add spinach and toss to combine.
3. Top salad with oranges and almonds.
4. Serve alongside any meat dish.

CRANBERRY-ALMOND BROCCOLI SALAD

Serves 8

Ingredients
- ¼ - cup finely chopped red onion
- 1/3 - cup canola mayonnaise
- 3 - tablespoons 2% reduced-fat Greek yogurt
- 1 - tablespoon cider vinegar
- 1 - tablespoon honey
- ¼ - teaspoon salt
- ¼ - teaspoon freshly ground black pepper
- 4 - cups coarsely chopped broccoli florets
- 1/3 - cup slivered almonds, toasted
- 1/3 - cup reduced-sugar dried cranberries
- 4 - center-cut bacon slices, cooked and crumbled

Instructions
1. Absorb red onion cold water for 5 minutes; channel.
2. Consolidate mayonnaise and then 5 fixings (through pepper), blending admirably with a whisk.
3. Mix in red onion, broccoli, and remaining fixings.
4. Spread and chill 1 hour before serving.

CRUNCHY ZUCCHINI CHIPS

Serves 4

Ingredients

- 1/3 - cup whole-wheat panko
- 3 - tablespoons uncooked amaranth
- ½ - teaspoon garlic powder
- ¼ - teaspoon kosher salt
- ¼ - teaspoon freshly ground black pepper
- 1 - ounce Parmesan cheese, finely grated
- 12 - ounces zucchini, cut into
- ¼ - inch-thick slices
- 1 - tablespoon olive oil Cooking spray

Instructions

1. Preheat stove to 425°. Join the initial 6 ingredients in a shallow dish. Join zucchini and oil in an enormous bowl; toss well to coat.
2. Dig zucchini in panko blend, squeezing tenderly to follow.
3. Spot covered cuts on an ovenproof wire rack covered with cooking shower; place the rack on a preparing sheet or jam move dish
4. Heat at 425° for 26 minutes or until cooked and fresh.
5. Serve chips right away.

GRILLED BROCCOLI

Serves 4 to 6

Ingredients
- 4 bunches of Broccoli
- 4 tbsp. Olive oil
- Black pepper and salt to taste
- ½ Lemon, the juice
- ½ Lemon cut into wedges

Instructions
1. Let the grill heat to High with closed lid.
2. In a bowl add the broccoli and drizzle with oil. Coat well. Season with salt.
3. Grill for 5 minutes and then flip. Cook for 3 minutes more.
4. Once done transfer on a plate.
5. Squeeze lemon on top and serve with lemon wedges.
6. Enjoy!

CAPRESE TOMATO SALAD

Serves 4

Ingredients
- 3 - cups halved multicolored cherry tomatoes
- 1/8 - teaspoon kosher salt
- ½ - cup fresh basil leaves
- 1 - tablespoon extra-virgin olive oil
- 1 - tablespoon balsamic vinegar
- ½ - teaspoon black pepper
- ¼ - teaspoon kosher salt
- 1 - ounce diced fresh mozzarella cheese (about 1/3 cup)

Instructions
1. Join tomatoes and 1/8 tsp. legitimate salt in an enormous bowl.
2. Let represent 5mins. Include basil leaves, olive oil, balsamic vinegar, pepper, 1/4 tsp. fit salt, and mozzarella; toss.

RASPBERRY AND BLUE CHEESE SALAD

Serves 4

Ingredients

- 1 ½ - tablespoons olive oil
- 1 ½ - teaspoons red wine vinegar
- ¼ - teaspoon Dijon mustard
- 1/8 - teaspoon salt
- 1/8 - teaspoon pepper
- 5 - cups mixed baby greens
- ½ - cup raspberries
- ¼ - cup chopped toasted pecans
- 1 - ounce blue cheese

Instructions

1. Join olive oil, vinegar, Dijon mustard, salt, and pepper.
2. Include blended infant greens; too.
3. Top with raspberries, walnuts, and blue cheddar.

ROASTED ASPARAGUS

Serves 4 to 6

Ingredients
- 1 bunch of Asparagus
- Salmon seasoning as needed
- 2 tbsp. Oil, or as needed

Instructions
1. Season the asparagus with salmon seasoning and drizzle with oil.
2. Make sure to coat well.
3. Let the grill heat to 350F with closed lid.
4. Grill the asparagus for 30 minutes.
5. Serve and enjoy!

WATERMELON-CUCUMBER SALAD

Serves 4

Ingredients
- 1 - tablespoon olive oil
- 2 - teaspoons fresh lemon juice
- ¼ - teaspoon salt
- 2 - cups cubed seedless watermelon
- 1 - cup thinly sliced English cucumber
- ¼ - cup thinly vertically sliced red onion
- 1 - tablespoon thinly sliced fresh basil

Instructions
1. Consolidate oil, squeeze, and salt in a huge bowl, mixing great.
2. Include watermelon, cucumber, and onion; toss well to coat.
3. Sprinkle plate of mixed greens equally with basil.

VERY POPULAR BBQ SAUCES
GRILLED RIBS

Serves 4

Ingredients
- 1 ½ kg one cut of ribs
- 1 tsp black pepper
- 1 tsp paprika
- 2 tsp garlic powder
- ¼ cup brown sugar
- 1 tsp salt
- ¼ cup BBQ sauce

Instructions
1. Prepare the ribs.
2. Trim the extra fat and cut the ribs.
3. Next, prepare the rub for the ribs.
4. In a bowl, mix the pepper, paprika, salt, garlic powder, brown sugar, and salt.
5. Rub this mixture on the ribs generously such that all parts of the ribs are rubbed with the herbs.
6. Put the ribs in a large zip lock bag and put them in the refrigerator overnight.
7. The next day, preheat the grill.
8. Bring out the ribs from the fridge and wait for them to get to room temperature.
9. Place the ribs on the grill and close the grill hood.
10. After 20 minutes, open the hood and turn the ribs and close the hood again.
11. Let the ribs grill for 20 more minutes.
12. Take the ribs out and let them rest for 5 minutes.
13. After that, enjoy the delicious ribs.

BBQ SMOKE RUBS

Serves 4

Ingredients
- 6 tablespoons brown sugar
- 2 tablespoons paprika
- 1 tablespoon salt
- 1 tablespoon ground black pepper
- 2 teaspoons garlic powder

Instructions
1. First, preheat the smoker grill at 225 degrees Fahrenheit, by closing the lid.
2. Mild wood chips can be used to create the smoke until the temperature is 100 degrees Fahrenheit.
3. Take a bowl and mix all the listed ingredients.
4. Transfer the bowl spices into an aluminum pie pan and place the pie pan directly onto the smoker grill grate and close the lid.
5. Smoke the spices for 2 hours.
6. Once done store in an air-tight glass jars for further use.

WORCE BEST BBQ SAUCE

Serves 3

Ingredients
- 1 small onion, finely chopped
- 2 garlic cloves, finely minced
- 2 cups ketchup
- 1 cup water
- ½ cup molasses
- ½ cup apple cider vinegar
- 5 tablespoons granulated sugar
- 5 tablespoons light brown sugar
- 1 tablespoon Worcestershire sauce
- 1 tablespoon freshly squeezed lemon juice
- 2 teaspoons liquid smoke
- 1½ teaspoons freshly ground black pepper
- 1 tablespoon yellow mustard

Instructions
1. On the stovetop, combine the onion, garlic, ketchup, water, molasses, apple cider vinegar, granulated sugar, brown sugar, Worcestershire sauce, lemon juice, liquid smoke, black pepper, and mustard.
2. Wait to boil, then reduce the heat to low and simmer for 30 minutes, straining out any bigger chunks, if desired.
3. If the sauce is cool completely then you can transfer to an airtight container and refrigerate for up to 2 weeks, or use a canning process to store for longer.

MIX VEGETABLES RUB

Serves 2

Ingredients
- 1 teaspoon freshly ground black pepper
- 1 teaspoon onion powder
- 1 teaspoon coarse kosher salt
- 1 teaspoon garlic powder
- 1 teaspoon sweet paprika
- ½ teaspoon cayenne pepper
- ½ teaspoon red pepper flakes
- ½ teaspoon dried oregano leaves
- ½ teaspoon dried thyme
- ½ teaspoon smoked paprika

Instructions
1. Using an airtight bag combine the black pepper, onion powder, salt, garlic powder, sweet paprika, cayenne, red pepper flakes, oregano, thyme, and smoked paprika.
2. Close the container and shake to mix.
3. Unused rub will keep in an airtight container for months.

SMOKED CHICKEN RUB

Serves 4

Ingredients
- 2 tablespoons packed light brown sugar
- 1½ teaspoons coarse kosher salt
- 1¼ teaspoons garlic powder
- ½ teaspoon onion powder
- ½ teaspoon freshly ground black pepper
- ½ teaspoon ground chipotle chili pepper
- ½ teaspoon smoked paprika
- ¼ teaspoon dried oregano leaves
- ¼ teaspoon mustard powder
- ¼ teaspoon cayenne pepper

Instructions
1. Using an airtight bag, combine the brown sugar, salt, garlic powder, onion powder, black pepper, chipotle pepper, paprika, oregano, mustard, and cayenne.
2. Close the container and shake to mix.
3. Unused rub will keep in an airtight container for months.

SEAFOOD RUB

Serves 2

Ingredients

- 2 tablespoons coarse kosher salt
- 2 tablespoons dried dill weed
- 1 tablespoon garlic powder
- 1½ teaspoons lemon pepper

Instructions

1. Using an airtight bag combine the salt, dill, garlic powder, and lemon pepper.
2. Close the container and shake to mix.
3. Unused rub will keep in an airtight container for months.

COFFEE BRISKET RUB

Serves 2

Ingredients

- 3 tablespoons coarse kosher salt
- 2 tablespoons ground espresso coffee
- 2 tablespoons freshly ground black pepper
- 1 tablespoon garlic powder
- 1 tablespoon light brown sugar
- 1½ teaspoons dried minced onion
- 1 teaspoon ground cumin

Instructions

1. Combine the salt, espresso, black pepper, garlic powder, brown sugar, minced onion, and cumin in a small airtight container or zip-top bag
2. Close the container and shake to mix.
3. Unused rub will keep in an airtight container for months.

NOT-JUST-FOR-PORK RUB

Serves 4

Ingredients
- ½ teaspoon ground thyme
- ½ teaspoon paprika
- ½ teaspoon coarse kosher salt
- ½ teaspoon garlic powder
- ½ teaspoon onion powder
- ½ teaspoon chili powder
- ¼ teaspoon dried oregano leaves
- ¼ teaspoon freshly ground black pepper
- ¼ teaspoon ground chipotle chili pepper
- ¼ teaspoon celery seed

Instructions
1. Using an airtight bag, combine the thyme, paprika, salt, garlic powder, onion powder, chili powder, oregano, black pepper, chipotle pepper, and celery seed.
2. Close the container and shake to mix.
3. Unused rub will keep in an airtight container for months.

QUEEN SPICE RUB

Serves 4

Ingredients

- 1 tablespoon salt
- 6 teaspoons ground cayenne pepper
- 6 teaspoons ground white pepper
- 2 teaspoons ground black pepper
- 4 teaspoons paprika
- 5 teaspoons onion powder
- 2 teaspoons garlic powder

Instructions

1. Preheat the smoker grill at 220 degrees Fahrenheit by closing the lid.
2. You can use apple wood chip to create the smoke.
3. The internal temperature should be 100 degrees Fahrenheit, to smoke the spices. Take a bowl and mix all the listed ingredients.
4. Transfer all the spices into aluminum pipe and place it on the grate.
5. Close the lid of the smoker and let it smoke for 1 hour.
6. Afterward, remove the foil tin from the grill and store in a tight jar for further use.

SWEET BROWN SUGAR RUB

Serves 4

Ingredients
- 2 tablespoons light brown sugar
- 1 teaspoon coarse kosher salt
- 1 teaspoon garlic powder
- 1 teaspoon onion powder
- 1 teaspoon sweet paprika
- ½ teaspoon freshly ground black pepper
- ½ teaspoon cayenne pepper
- ½ teaspoon dried oregano leaves
- ¼ teaspoon smoked paprika

Instructions
1. Combine the brown sugar, salt, garlic powder, onion powder, sweet paprika, black pepper, cayenne, oregano, and smoked paprika in a small airtight container or zip-top bag
2. Close the container and shake to mix.
3. Unused rub will keep in an airtight container for months.

SWEET AND SPICY CINNAMON RUB

Serves 3

Ingredients
- 2 tablespoons light brown sugar
- 1 teaspoon coarse kosher salt
- 1 teaspoon garlic powder
- 1 teaspoon onion powder
- 1 teaspoon sweet paprika
- ½ teaspoon freshly ground black pepper
- ½ teaspoon cayenne pepper
- ½ teaspoon dried oregano leaves
- ½ teaspoon ground ginger
- ½ teaspoon ground cumin
- ¼ teaspoon smoked paprika
- ¼ teaspoon ground cinnamon
- ¼ teaspoon ground coriander
- ¼ teaspoon chili powder

Instructions
1. Using an airtight bag, combine the brown sugar, salt, garlic powder, onion powder, sweet paprika, black pepper, cayenne, oregano, ginger, cumin, smoked paprika, cinnamon, coriander, and chili powder.
2. Close the container and shake to mix.
3. Unused rub will keep in an airtight container for months.

THREE PEPPER RUB

Serves 3

Ingredients
- 2 tablespoons of black pepper
- 2 tablespoons of white pepper
- 2 tablespoons of red pepper
- 1 tablespoon of onion powder
- 2 teaspoons of garlic powder
- 2 tablespoons of dried thyme
- 4 tablespoons of paprika
- 2 tablespoons of dried oregano

Instructions
1. Mix all the spices in the bowl and transfer to aluminum foil tin.
2. Preheat the smoker grill at 220 degrees F for 20 minutes.
3. Put the aluminum foil tin onto the grill grate and smoke for 3 hours by closing the lid.
4. Once done, store it in the tight jar for further use.

NOTES

CPSIA information can be obtained
at www.ICGtesting.com
Printed in the USA
BVHW011215180521
607638BV00007B/778